The
THEREFORE
of Marriage

GOD'S DESIGN + OPERATIONAL PROTOCOL

AYO OLALEYE

Chicago | Lagos | Ontario

The Therefore of Marriage: *God's Design + Operational* Protocol©
AYO OLALEYE

ISBN: 978-1-7377864-1-2

Cover Photo: MidoDezines
Content Editor: Sherilynn Asuoha | 7th Seal Advantage
Copy Editor: Olubukola Adebayo | Ariwa Consulting

Published by 7th Seal Advantage Publishing, LLC

First Printing Edition, 2021

To Jesus, my Savior and Lord.

Of Your fullness, Lord, I have received grace upon grace.

Including the blessing of Titilope as my wife.

...

TABLE OF CONTENT

ACKNOWLEDGEMENTS

"Now to Him who is able to do so much more than all we ask or imagine, according to His power that is at work within us, to Him be the glory in the church and in Christ Jesus throughout all generations, forever and ever. Amen."
Ephesians 3:20-21

Several people have been instrumental to my Christian pilgrimage. It will be difficult to mention them all, but these few names come readily to mind: Bro Gbile & Sis Sade Akanni, Late Professor Zacharias Tanee Fomum, Gary Thomas, John Piper, and Dr. Ferdinand Nweke. I also thank God for His grace and the privilege of fellowship and service at the Baptist Student Fellowship, especially the Ogun Conference BSF (OGBSF) and BSFFPI.

I am grateful to God for the nurturing I've received from my parents, Rev. Layi & Mrs Hannah Adunni Olaleye, Pastor and Mrs. Kola Alabi, Mama Bolajoko Adeyemi, and Mama Victoria Ojo (a.k.a Mama Kaduna). Your prayer and support as I follow God's call are valued beyond words. A special thank you to my Pastor, Rev. Dr. Israel Akanji.

Numerous people were used of God to nudge and encourage me to work on this book: Pastor Tayo Oladipo, Bro. Gbenga Adedokun, and

Pastor Timothy Adeyemo of Kingdom Noble Church, who gladly gave me his pulpit where most of the truth herein was first shared. Some of those messages were transcribed forming much of this book's content.

My colleagues at Olaleye Olatunji & Partners, Opemipo Olatunji and Enitan Ekanem, were usually the first recipients of my thoughts. Thank you for providing me the opportunity to rub minds with you.

Mrs. Bukola Dayo-Adebayo, thank you for your commitment to this writing. Your coming on board FRM oiled the wheel of this project and many more. You injected your editorial skills into the raw manuscript and gave it structure. Barr. Sola Adekanye, Mrs Bukola Babalola, and Mrs. Louis Ricket, who transcribed and compiled the earliest stages of content, thank you. Opemipo Olatunji, thank you for reading through the first manuscript and doing much of structural arrangement. Mrs. Sherilynn Asuoha of 7th Seal Advantage, thank you for beautifying this project with your content editorial skill. God bless your great heart.

I appreciate all the leaders, workers, volunteers, and the entire Family Resource Ministry (FRM) team. Thank you for your labor of love in working towards fulfilling the FRM mandate.

Thank you, Dcn. Dr. Tunde Oluwatola, Pastor Kola Alabi, Pastor Sunday Oluwaleye (CLAM), Rev. William Abadoo, Elders Bill & Shirley Stewart, Dr. Ted Rendall, and my brothers: Tunji Adeniran, Wole Olabanji, Ayo Banjoko, Taiwo Osho, and Bayo Adekanmbi for proofreading this work at short notice. Your thoughts and suggestions are invaluable. Dimeji & Tokunbo Ogunleye, thank you for your commitment to the brotherhood we share and for your support on this project.

I appreciate my siblings, family, and friends who have stood with me and by me through prayers and counsel on this road of following God's call.

Lastly and most importantly, to my wife, Titilope, who nudged and spurred me into this writing, and our children- your love is unquantifiable. Thank you for loving me sacrificially.

INTRODUCTION

O ne morning, I was ready to go out. I got into my car. I placed my keys in the ignition. I turned my key, but car refused to start. *Perhaps there is a problem with my battery*, I thought. Thankfully, I had a jumper cable, and my wife was yet to take her leave. It gave me time to use her car to jump my own. I drove her car close enough to mine so I could use my jumper cable to connect the two batteries.

I place one end of the jumper cable to my battery. Success. As I placed the other end on the cable to my wife's battery, there was a spark. Uh oh. I realized I wrongly connected the positive from my wife's battery to the negative of mine. The jumper cable could not serve me as long as I had the wrong connection. I made the necessary correction and eventually, I got my car started. Everything was good now. Or so I thought. It was then that I realized damage had already taken place. The jumper cable was good, but I wrongly deployed it. So instead of it being a help, it ended up causing damage to my car.

Marriage is God's vision; it is God's design. It is God's unique help to mankind. God designed marriage to be a blessing but unfortunately, many people's experiences do not attest to this beautiful provision of God. There is a visible disconnect between God's offering and our experience in practice because many people are living far below God's plan for marriage.

It is certain that this disconnect emanates from us and not from God, for God does not lie. The alarming, increasing rate of dysfunctionality in marriage is a result of the fact that *"all of us, like sheep have strayed away. We have left God's path to follow our own"* Isaiah 53:6 (NLT). The problem is clearly a case of a lack of understanding of God's design for marriage and a lack of acceptance and/or adherence to the protocols that come with the design.

This book is focused on these two – the design and the protocols of marriage as intended by God from scriptures. The first part focuses on deepening understanding of the design of marriage, while the second part focuses on the operational protocols.

As you read through, you may find certain things confronting your age-long beliefs; some of them might make you uncomfortable and challenge your norm. However, be open-minded and evaluate them in the light of God's word, not your experience or culture, and definitely not the world's standard. Why? *"The world and its desire passes away but only those who do the will of God abides forever.[1]"*

In writing this book, I do not project myself as one who is perfect on the subject matter because fulfilling God's plan is a process, not a destination. My marriage with Titilope is still a work in progress, a

---

[1] I John 2:17

growing one; we are learning daily to conform our lives and marriage to God's pattern more and more. His grace has been graciously lavished on us.

It is not an attempt to express my views or opinions, but a desire to further deepen the understanding of God's word on the subject of marriage, to help you catch a bigger vision of what God had in mind when He initiated marriage. Times and seasons change, cultures differ from place to place, opinions and views about issues differ from person to person. We all have different backgrounds and exposure, but the word of God is eternal and changes not with times and seasons.

I send this book out with prayers, that God will use it for His glory in the transformation of marriages, including yours in Jesus' name. May your marriage become a vivid picture and model of God's heartbeat for marriage. Amen.

Part One

THE DESIGN

THE DESIGN

God designed marriage. He conceived it. He created it to look and operate as He desired. It is His initiative, His handiwork. Think about choosing to purchase the car of your dreams. Once you pay the price and sign the papers, the car is yours, yes? But what makes the car work and what attracted you to buy it in the first place is already designed and established.

Can you make modifications to the car? Yes, within reason and according to the manufacturer's recommendations and standards. Once you begin to make modifications to the car that are not recommended by the vehicles' manufacturer, it does not matter how convenient or enjoyable the alterations are to you, you run the risk of malfunctions and lesser performance because you are operating outside of the manufacturer's intention and design for that vehicle.

As with any creation, one cannot ignore design and the designer and expect that creation to yield optimal results. In fact, when you fail to clearly understand the purpose and design of a thing, you are guaranteed to abuse it, because you don't know how to use it properly. Try as you may, you can never enjoy the best of a product that you do not understand. Nothing works well outside of its design. This book is designed to educate you on the "therefore" of marriage. We will talk more about that as time progresses. First, let's spend some time on design.

Divorce rates are what they are today, largely because we have decided to make things work our way. It's our marriage, right? Why can't we make it work with our own conditions and standards? Marriage is, in fact, designed to work for us. But the only way we can ever obtain the maximum benefits of marriage is by aligning ourselves with the Manufacturer of the marriage covenant - God. Understand that to get married is to enter into an institution that has already been configured. Your role is simply to operate in line with the Manufacturer's intent.

For the sake of clarity, let us dissect the meaning of the term "design". Designs are constructed to customize experiences. They promote functionality (www.businessdictionary.com). When something is designed, it creates the opportunity for a pattern. God, Creator of the Universe, designed marriage to be something a lot bigger than your wedding day. It is an institution He deemed necessary for the well-being of mankind on this side of eternity.

A lot of marriages fail today because husbands and wives have yet to take time to review the marriage contract or consult the Manufacturer. They do not take time to follow the manual for optimal performance. The Bible is the ultimate manual for marriage, and it must be followed if we will make the most of our marriages. Husbands and wives are at their best and enjoy true fulfillment when they walk in line with God's design for marriage. This section of the book unpacks the principles, problems, and biblical recommendations for resolve. Be blessed as you read!

CHAPTER ONE
THE THEREFORE

The Lord God said, "It is not good for the man to be alone....
Genesis 2:1

There is one truth we will need to establish before we delve into the topic of marriage. Everything God created is good. He said so Himself. He took the time to assess every work of Creation, by Himself, and the verdict was always good.

For example, God carefully examined the final product of all His activities on Day One of creation. Upon taking it all in, He determined all was good and declared it so (Genesis 1:3). Nothing about His process of evaluation and declaration changed when it came to making man, except that when He looked at the man that He created and breathed life into, along with all He had done, He decided it was "very good" (Genesis 1:31). Is that not great? Every man was created for a great purpose by a great God to do great things on the earth.

THE PROBLEM

After creating Adam, God discovered something that was not good. For the first time, God said, "It is not good…" What was not good? Man… alone (Gen 2:18). The man himself was not bad at all. Do not forget, man was created in the image of God and God is good. We also know that it had nothing to do with his capacity because we saw God immediately put man to work by allowing him to name all the animals.

What was not good was the identified problem of Adam's aloneness. Adam was separated from others. He was different from the rest of creation. There was God, there were animals and there were plants, but Adam was alone in his class. The animals existed in different kinds and were in pairs. God existed in Triune: Father, Son, and Holy Spirit. After God brought all the animals before Adam to name, it was observed that for

Every man was created for a great purpose by a great God to do great things on the earth.

Adam, no suitable helper was found (Genesis 2:20). He was alone in his class. Loneliness is a problem, but literally being alone is a far worse burden. Again, nothing was wrong with the man. Rather, it can be safely inferred that the "not good" declaration had to do with the fact that man could not fully express his person in his alone state. God created man in His image.

… and God said, "Let us make man in our image…".

-Genesis 1:26, KJV-

Man was designed to reflect the relational aspect or nature of God who exists in three persons: Father, Son, and Holy Spirit. Man was created as a relational being, just like God, and as such, his being could only be fully expressed in relationships. By extension, our sense of fulfillment lies in relating with other people because that is how we were designed to function. It is also important to note that when God said that 'it is not good for man to be alone', the declaration was not solely for Adam, but humans in general. God, in His wisdom, saw that life would be so much better with a helper-companion.

GOD'S RESPONSE: THE SOLUTION

"I will make a helper suitable for him."

-Genesis 2:18b-

In response to this aloneness challenge, God made woman. He took from that which He already made – man – to form her. This act confirms the completion and perfection status of the original man because it wouldn't have made any sense to make up for a deficiency from the deficient product. It wouldn't have made sense to make up for the aloneness of Adam by taking from the same Adam if Adam was not already a perfect being. The first man was complete and perfect in himself as God's image and as God intended. God, in solving the problem of aloneness, chose, in so many words, to split the excellent work into two

> Our sense of fulfillment lies in relating with other people because that is how we were designed to function.

so that the original one man who was complete and perfect could now manifest on two fronts.

The Bible records that God put Adam to sleep and took from his bone, closed it up with flesh and fashioned into a woman, the rib which was taken from him (Gen 2:21-22). The word translated 'rib' was used about thirty-five (35) times in the Old Testament; however, apart from this one time, no other time was it interpreted to mean 'rib.' In about twenty (20) instances, it was translated side (Exodus 25:12, 14; 26:20, 26-27). Adam further affirmed this saying:

"This is now bone of my bones and flesh of my flesh; she shall be called 'woman,' for she was taken out of man."

- Genesis 2:23-

This woman was taken out of the man and as such, she is part of the man. For this reason, she was named "Woman". Therefore, by definition, origin, source, and name, the woman is essentially a part of the man. She was not created from the dust like man, but from man. All the female parts of the man were pulled out, put together as one, and became known as "Woman".

THE CHALLENGE FROM THE SOLUTION

God, in proffering a solution to the 'aloneness of the man,' decided to take something away from the original man to create a woman. As the original man has been split into two: man and woman, we cannot say that the new man is still in the actual state and status of the original man because something has been taken away from him that is now standing as the woman. This 'surgical' operation carried out by God left the two persons incomplete individually. Neither of them could claim the originality of the first man on their own without the other.

There is something in the original man that is now not in the man but in the woman. And there is something in the initial man that the woman still doesn't have, but now only in the new man. So, none can express the fullness and capacity of the first man without the other. Each part is not a complete individual part of the whole man - the original man. So neither the man nor the woman has the capacity and component of the initial man. Each part is deficient in a way because there is now a part of him or her in the other.

THE THEREFORE

"Therefore, shall a man leave his father and his mother, and shall cleave unto his wife: and they shall be one flesh"

-Genesis 2:24, KJV-

Marriage, therefore, is God's way of restoring man to his original state and form, but in harmony, just as God exists within Himself.

The reason a man and a woman will cleave to each other as husband and wife is because the woman was part of the man ab-initio; she is the bone of his bone and the flesh of his flesh. God's idea of marriage is to bring back together, two parts that were formerly one entity before the operation. Marriage, therefore, is God's way of restoring man to his original state and form, but in harmony, just as God exists within Himself.

Let's talk about the "therefore," or the "why" of marriage for a moment. "Therefore, for this reason... "For this cause," ... "That is why," and "This explains why," are opening statements used in the various Biblical translations of Genesis 2:24.

Why does a man need to leave his father and mother, and be united with his wife to become 'one?' Why do they need to return to their original state after being made male and female? It is because she is the 'bone of his bone, the flesh of his flesh'. It is because that was how they were before and that is the way to return to their originally intended state and capacity. So, one major purpose of marriage is restoration. It is in the union of husband and wife that what was removed is restored and initial capacity, regained. This is the 'therefore' of marriage. This is the 'why'.

CHAPTER TWO

THE IMPLICATION

The Lord God said, "It is not good for the man
to be alone....
-Genesis 2:1-

God gave Adam divine anesthesia as He removed a piece of his God-like perfection to form the woman. This procedure-the splitting of Adam into two entities, Adam and Eve-resulted in having two individuals who were incomplete on their own. God's solution to the problem of aloneness created a challenge: neither Adam nor Eve could claim the originality of the first man on their own. They needed each other. Now, there are two implications to this that we must discuss in-depth:

- The implication of capacity
- The implication of components

CAPACITY

Capacity has everything to do with how far you can go in life. It is the measure of your ability to get things done. The extent of your ability to produce, contain, retain, understand, and perform are all demonstrations of your capacity. If ever it is said about you that you lack the capacity to accomplish something, what they are really saying about you is that you do not have what it takes to carry out the assignment in question. May you always have the capacity to do that which God has called you to do in the mighty name of Jesus.

As much as we should all aspire to increase in capacity and do all we can do, it is not everything on earth that we were programmed to do and not by ourselves. God, in His generous mercy, gives us the talent, access, and calling according to our capacity. We observe in the Gospel of Matthew chapter twenty-five as Jesus tells us the story of the stewards and the talents, that assignments and responsibilities are usually given in consideration with one's capacity. To accept responsibility above one's capacity is to be programmed for failure, just as extending a task to a person that is below his or her capability is a waste of resources.

> Capacity has everything to do with how far you can go in life. It is the measure of your ability to get things done.

In the Genesis account, Adam was given assignments and responsibilities based on his capacity before the woman was formed. The Lord took Adam, placed him in the Garden of Eden to tend it, and commanded him,

"You are free to eat from any tree in the garden; but you must not eat from the tree of the knowledge of good and evil, for when you eat of it you will surely die." The Lord God said, "It is not good for the man to be alone. I will make a helper suitable for him."

-Genesis 2:15-18, -

The task of naming all the animals was also in line with Adam's capacity. God placing Adam in the garden, giving him instructions on what to eat and what not to eat, and authorizing him to name all the animals and cultivate the garden was evidence of man's capacity to produce and cultivate. As much as Adam could do all these independently, there was an aspect of godliness he did not have the capacity to achieve alone. This is why God said his aloneness was not good. Adam had so many godly features on the inside, but God saw something that was critical enough for Him to speak out about and devise a plan to resolve because anything less than 'good' is less than God and that would decrease Adam's capacity.

When something is perfect, it means that it is all that it should be. For instance, if a tiny part is removed from a perfect machine, it stops working seamlessly. It could even begin to malfunction and cause damage to other components. A gadget can only fully perform the function it was made for when all of its components are complete and working together.

A gadget can only fully perform the function it was made for when all of its components are complete and working together.

Since something was already removed from the original man to make the woman, it followed that the man no longer had the same capacity he had before. The new man could not have retained the initial ability because when something is perfect, it means that it is all that it should be. Adam could no longer deliver maximally all that the Maker had in mind originally because he was no longer in the initial state he was made.

When God created the original man, in him was both the maleness and femaleness, like a hermaphrodite (Gen 1:27). In the initial man, I imagine there was a womb to carry a pregnancy, and man, on his own, could bring the egg and fertilize it just in himself. I imagine that the reason why we still have animal hermaphrodites, such as snails, is to serve as a witness to this possibility. Even some plants have both male and female reproductive parts. The "femaleness" in man was taken away from Adam to create the woman.

Hence, we can safely infer that the reproductive organs were a whole in the original man. The one we now referred to as the female reproductive organ is the part that was removed from the man to make the woman. The eggs came to the woman and the sperm to fertilize remained with the man. This arrangement implies that the reproductive organs will always need each other to fulfill their purpose. To achieve reproduction, for the blessing of the womb to come to reality, the male reproductive organ needs the female reproductive organ. Both parties must agree; they must come together as one entity. This same principle applies in every other aspect of married life. Now, why not leave them as one?

Then God blessed them, and God said to them, "Be fruitful and multiply; fill the earth and subdue it; have dominion over the fish of the sea, over the birds of the air, and over every living thing that moves on the earth."

-Genesis 1:28, NKJV-

We can see the same amplified in the relationship between Christ and the Church, which is a model of marriage. Christ is not fully expressed. His power, His glory is not fully expressed without

the Church. The manifestation of Christ's power and glory on earth is limited to the extent to which the Church is ready to manifest it. The Church is nothing without Christ. This model is the pattern for the husband and the wife. Like

> The manifestation of Christ's power and glory on earth is limited to the extent to which the Church is ready to manifest it.

Adam, Christ sees the beauty and glory of the Church- which is His body- as a piece pulled out of Himself, called to partner with Him to be fruitful and multiply so that God's kingdom will be established on the earth!

When a whole is separated into parts, each part of the whole becomes deficient one way or the other. Each piece of the whole cannot be said to be sufficient on its own. The other part will always be needed to make for proper functioning.

Because the responsibility was given based on the original capacity of Adam, there was no way he could have successfully cultivated and kept the garden without Eve. His ability to fulfill God's purpose or assignment was much dependent on him getting back what was removed from him.

This understanding should thus cut out all forms of competition between husband and wife. The question should be, "Who is going to bring the best result for a particular task?" and you just go ahead to get it sorted. The reason we compete, and fight is that, often, we do not view marriage the way God intended it to be. Husband and wife were never designed to run on their own. They can only fulfill the purpose of marriage, as intended by God, by seeing and treating themselves as one body.

> The husband and wife were never designed to run on their own. They can only fulfill the purpose of marriage, as intended by God, by seeing and treating themselves as one body.

COMPONENTS

So, the Lord God caused the man to fall into a deep sleep. While the man slept, the Lord God took out one of the man's ribs and closed up the opening. Then the Lord God made a woman from the rib, and he brought her to the man. "This is it!" Adam exclaimed. "She is part of my own bone and flesh!"

-Genesis 2:23, TLB-

A component is a part or element of a larger whole, a constituent part; something belonging together. From the divine operation through which the woman was formed, we can safely deduce that husband and wife are a part of each other, different components of a single entity just as we discussed in the previous segment. As soon as Adam saw the woman, he identified her and quickly confirmed this truth (Genesis 2:23). His reaction proves that everything in Eve was taken from Adam, meaning that the woman is part and parcel of the man.

The attributes displayed in the woman are the ones taken from the man and what we see in the man are the features left in there, not taken out. If Eve was beautiful, it means that her beauty was derived from Adam. If Eve was fair in complexion, even though Adam was dark-complexioned, it means that this complexion existed in the original and was transferred to the woman.

It is also safe to infer that whatever weakness or strength is seen in Eve was derived from Adam. The man is fully responsible for whatever is found in the woman because it is from him that the woman was taken; he is her source.

"For the man did not come from woman but woman from man"

-1 Corinthians 11:8-

Indeed, if the woman is Adam's bone and flesh, whatever is seen in the woman is from the man. If a man thinks his wife is foolish, then it is likely that it is the dumb part of him that was removed that is functioning in his wife. If a man says to his wife that she looks like a monkey, what he is saying, invariably, is that he is the monkey because she is *"part of his own flesh and blood"*. So, the implication of being a component of one another is that you are of the same source.

When you split something into two, there may be a part of the whole in one half and a different part in the other half. This means that it is possible that one part has some strength, and the other part may exhibit a lack of it. In the context of marriage, the things you complain of and fight your partner over, are usually those things that are your area of strength and your spouse's place of weakness, or the reverse.

Since the two formed the whole originally, if much is taken to a part, automatically the other part will be less. So, for equilibrium to occur, you must bring the two together again in the married life. If a couple is made of the same component, then caution and sensitivity should be exercised to take responsibility because that is what marriage is designed to be.

Your responsibility is to use your 'less' to balance out your spouses 'more'. You should see your spouse as part of you. If my left hand drops a phone and the phone is broken, I was the one that broke the phone because my left hand is part of me; it is one body. It is only a lack of this understanding that would make me say that my left hand is responsible.

Let me attempt to illustrate my point with a personal experience. Some time ago, I was using a phone from one of the famous brands and it was quite expensive to change the screen. Sadly, I had changed the screen so many times that I vowed never to use that brand of phone again. On this particular night, my wife and kids were with the phone and then the screen broke again. I was so unhappy that I went on and on about how the whole situation could have been prevented if my wife had been more careful. I eventually fixed it after some days.

> If a couple is made of the same component, then caution and sensitivity should be exercised to take responsibility because that is what marriage is designed to be.

The following day after fixing the phone, I went on a prayer walk at noon and I couldn't even explain how the phone dropped. Anyway, the screen broke again. Although I was shocked and unhappy, I was very eager to fix it immediately because I had no one to blame – not my left hand or right hand that dropped the phone. I took responsibility and replaced it immediately without anyone's knowledge. However, when it involved my wife, I was quick to apportion blame and see what she could have done differently

If I understood that we were part of a whole, I would not rejoice in blaming her, with the consideration that it could have been me in that situation. Besides, my wife is truly a part of me, so I should take things in stride, and together with her, seek a solution to the issue.

When we understand this, we will learn to take responsibility for each other because that is how it is meant to be. As components, you and your spouse are not the same, but different parts of a single entity. You are a part of each other.

CHAPTER THREE

THE JOINING

The man said, "This is now bone of my bones and flesh of my flesh; she shall be called 'woman,' for she was taken out of man." For this reason, a man will leave his father and mother and be united to his wife, and they will become one flesh. The man and his wife were both naked, and they were not ashamed.
-Genesis 2:23-25, BSB-

There is a general misconception that marriage is an equal partnership; a give-and-take; a 50/50 arrangement. However, a closer look at scriptures will tell us that this is very far from the truth. Marriage is not a partnership affair because partnership suggests a transactional relationship - you put in a part and your spouse puts in a part, in a specific ratio, for example, 50:50, no more, no less on either side. On the contrary, biblical marriage is not putting in a part, but putting in all. The understanding of marriage as a partnership affair is not in line with the scriptural description of marriage.

"So, they are no longer two, but one flesh. Therefore, what God has joined together, let no one separate."

-Matthew 19:6-

According to Scriptures, marriage requires that each person lays down his or her all. Its description, according to God's idea, is that of joining to become a single entity.

"For this reason, a man will leave his father and mother and be united to his wife and the two will become one flesh. So, they are no longer two, but one flesh. Therefore, what God has joined together, let no one separate."

-Mark 10:7-9-

COMPONENTS OF JOINING

INPUT: A male and a female. God designed marriage to join a male and female to become husband and wife, one flesh.

OUTCOME: This joining makes the two-a male and a female- become 'one flesh'. When the two are joined, they are no longer two but one.

According to Scriptures, marriage requires that each person lays down his or her all.

REQUIREMENT: The joining requires separation from others for proper cleaving to take place.

RESULT: The two persons, who have become one, share and bear with each other; and become stronger and better. They become more useful and productive. Two are better than one.

FEATURES OF JOINING IN RELATION TO MARRIAGE

Joining is an underlying principle of biblical marriage. Joining requires the two individuals who are entering the marital relationship to lose their individuality. They can no longer operate as separate individuals but can only function effectively as a single entity.

The marital union is sure to go defunct if husband and wife attempt to operate outside of the principle of joining. The reason is that their functionality as individuals will only end up short-changing them because their outcome will always be only a fraction of what is achievable by their joint efforts. Marriage takes away your individuality, leading to interdependence. There are no longer two entities, only one flesh - a married couple. Neither person can function as a separate entity and operate maximally.

"… and the two will become one flesh. So they are no longer two, but one flesh."

-Mark 10:8-

When you get married, God expects your functionality as a single entity. His disposition to you becomes, as it were, toward a single individual. For instance, He no longer blesses either the husband or the wife, He blesses the family. The husband or the wife becomes only a channel through which the blessings flow.

When He gives the couple an assignment, He expects to see the two working together to achieve it as it becomes impossible for only one of them to accomplish the task as intended by God. I do not mean to say one person cannot achieve anything without the input of the other. Given God's grace available to the couple, whatever an individual achieves outside the cooperation of his or her spouse is only a fraction of what is possible. They can no longer carry out any responsibility attached to their union at their best when they are not in cooperation.

For instance, parenting as a responsibility of marriage cannot be achieved to the utmost by a single parent. With due respect to hardworking single parents around the world, I do not intend to demean your efforts. I only mean to say, in God's estimation, your best efforts can only achieve a fraction of what is achievable compared with if your spouse plays his or her part under God.

Someone might say, "Considering the way Mrs. A raised her son and what she has accomplished with him, many couples with good marriage could not even boast of having such great parenting experience and results." I agree that this is possible by God filling the gap if the single parent is an elect of God, but even at that, what God would do through the force of two partners would not be comparable (Ecclesiastes 4:9).

Marriage takes away your individuality, leading to interdependence

How about the widows and those called to celibacy, eunuchs? My submission is that these circumstances come with grace as stated by the Bible in the gospel of Matthew 19:11-12. God, Himself, fills this space and role in such lives. He said of the widows that He is their Defender and Sustainer. The Psalmist wrote,

"The Lord … sustains the fatherless and the widow..."

-Psalms 146:9a-

Indeed, God is the husband of widows.

When things are joined together, their union becomes stronger and of greater value than the individual components. The value and power of a team cannot be downplayed in any circle- not in businesses, not in the local or universal church, and definitely not in marriage. Two are always better than one.

There is minimal use for the handle of a mug when it is operating separately from the mug. Likewise, a mug without its handle is only a cup with limitations on what it can actually bear. But when the two components are put together, they provide a stronger vessel, more useful, and more convenient to use, compared to their separate functionalities.

"Two are better than one, because they have a good return for their labor"

-Ecclesiastes 4:9-

Every joining has a purpose. In marriage, the couple fulfills the purpose of joining only when they remain together. When you join forces as a couple, you are more potent in fulfillment of purpose.

Components joined together inherit both the assets and liabilities of the individual members. Also, in the marriage context, each partner inherits the assets and liabilities of the other person. A couple shares both blessings and curses in the lives of the partner they are joined with. Marriage brings together both the good and the bad of the two individuals. If a car, possessing a speed of 200km/hr., is joined to a truck, it can no longer run at that speed because the truck to which it is joined has no capacity for such speed. The two parties must know what they are entering into so that they can learn how to deal with it. Because marriage is a joining, the two lives and the two destinies are joined together.

When things are joined together, it is difficult to separate them successfully. It becomes 'we' not 'me'. When what is bound is separated, it loses its purpose. The only way to fulfill their common goal and purpose is to keep them intact. When a chair is dismantled, each component loses its value. Their original value as a united entity is lost and as individuals, each part reduces in value.

Marriage separation is described as 'broken' because you cannot separate two people who are joined in marriage without causing injuries.

You've heard the phrase, *broken marriage*, yes? Marriage separation is described as 'broken' because you cannot separate two people who are joined in marriage without causing injuries. Just as a human body is one whole entity and cannot function effectively when divided, marriage is a joining into one single entity and functions optimally when the couple operates as one; therein lies their fulfillment.

Part Two

THE PROTOCOL

WHAT IS PROTOCOL?

The amount of breakage, collapse, and confusion that exists in our world today is almost unfathomable. The fragmented state of our society and of the general state of marriages across the globe has less to do with its fragility and more to do with the recognition of and adherence to protocol.

You may know the term, "protocol" from church or your place of work. Generally speaking, protocol is a determination of the 'who', 'what', 'when', and 'how' of the interrelation of multiple parts. For example, the different pieces of metal working together as a machine or a team of people working on a project in an office both require a protocol that is understood by all components if they are to function properly.

But let's examine this word in its technical context. Science recognizes "protocol" as a form of data transmission. According to the Oxford Language Dictionary, it is the exchange of information between at least two automated or electronically-driven devices.

The principle of protocol, according to data science and analytics, asserts that effective exchanges of information between two or more entities require a pre-existing agreement as to how said information must be structured and how it must function to effectively send and receive relevant signals and commands. When protocol is not adhered to, a defect is sure.

For instance, the terminals in a socket are distinct from one another and must stay this way to avoid surge issues. One cannot do the work of the other. Why? They are not designed to perform the same functions, though they exist in the same space. Per adventure they need to interact to achieve a specific purpose, protocol exists to allow this to happen safely and effectively.

Outside of computer and data science, protocol exists to provide order, especially as it pertains to communication and engagement in a specific society, organization, or institution. The establishment of protocol prevents disorderliness and chaos and promotes productivity and efficiency.

In marriage, protocol exists to ensure harmony. This is a truth that is often ignored or that many simply are not aware of despite how critical it is for a successful marriage. Protocol is so important that when it is not adhered to, problems automatically arise, impacting not only the participating entities but the environment as well.

CHAPTER FOUR

WHY PROTOCOL IN MARRIAGE?

"But if I am delayed, I write so that you may know how you ought to conduct yourself in the house of God, which is the church of the living God, the pillar and ground of the truth."
1 Timothy 3:15, NKJV

The essence of protocol is not hierarchy, importance, or superiority, but orderliness. One of the reasons so many marriages are breaking up is attributed to a lack of adherence to the protocols of marriage as designed by God. The husband wants to take on the role of the wife while the wife wants to assume a role designed for her husband.

The effect of shifting roles is tantamount to putting two live wires together. You will get a spark because they are not meant to be placed together. If one of the ports of a socket is not working, supplying live or negative current and the other is functioning correctly, the socket will not perform as designed. The negative is as important as the positive; the absence of one renders the other ineffective. You cannot have both ports supplying positives and negatives just because they can. They must assume their distinct roles to do well.

It is wrong to believe, as some people do, that the man is more important than the woman because they are both equally as important. God made things, including marriage, to work efficiently through an established protocol. Each partner has a specific role assigned to them and things will only work well when each person rightfully occupies their position. They were not made to compete with each other.

In the socket illustration, each port is satisfied doing what it was designed to do and as they are doing it, the socket delivers. If either of them fails to carry out their respective functions, the socket fails. An order exists that allows each piece to perform its assigned task; the protocol is displayed in the order of arrangement of the joint work.

> The essence of protocol is not hierarchy, importance, or superiority, but orderliness.

One of the beautiful things about watching a military parade is the order. If a few of them decide to move their legs only when they want, there will be disorder and the beauty will be lost. The order in which they flow is governed by the protocol they follow, and this is what yields beauty. The same thing applies to marriage: when order is missing, there is confusion, and the expected beauty is lost.

Let's talk for a moment about the protocol of the Godhead, otherwise known as the Trinity. They are one God, but there is an order: Father, Son, and Holy Spirit. Because of this set order, Jesus said He does nothing on His own, though the Bible makes it clear that Jesus is God Himself. Jesus is not lower in rank, but He understands order.

All through Scriptures, anywhere God brings two or more persons to work on the same assignment, He introduces order in the form of role and hierarchy. Some examples are:

- Moses and Aaron: *"Aaron will be your spokesman to the people. He will be your mouthpiece, and you will stand in the place of God for him, telling him what to say" Exodus 4:16 NLT*
- Bezalel and Oholiab: *"And I have personally appointed Oholiab son of Ahisamach, of the tribe of Dan, to be his assistant. Moreover, I have given special skill to all the gifted craftsmen so they can make all the things I have commanded you to make" Exodus 31:6, NLT*
- Paul and Barnabas: *"Barnabas they called Zeus, and Paul they called Hermes because he was the chief speaker" Acts 14:12, NIV*
- The Trinity: God the Father, God the Son, God the Holy Spirit.

The same thing happens in marriage, God's divine institution made especially for us. When protocol is adhered to, confusion is removed, and the evidence or outcome is beauty (Ephesians 5:22-29).

Every gadget comes with a manufacturer's manual and we, as users, are constrained to operate and use the device according to the manufacturer's manual. Even though I bought a phone with my money, my right over it is, to an extent, restricted by the designer's prescription, if it will fulfill the purpose of its existence.

I don't have the freedom to decide that because it is my phone, I will go into the swimming pool with it. I cannot choose that instead of charging the phone in the electric socket, I will power it with the gas hose. If I decide to drive on it, I

> All through Scriptures, anywhere God brings two or more persons to work on the same assignment, He introduces order in the form of role and hierarchy

am deciding to abuse the gadget because I am treating it contrary to what the designer had in mind. I cannot choose to use my phone outside what is permitted by the designer and still expect to enjoy its maximum benefits. God created marriage and it can only work productively when we implement it according to the way it is designed to function.

Ignoring the manufacturer's prescription usually results in the malfunctioning of the product. It will be foolish to think that we can make the best of our matrimony if we choose to ignore the Designer's instructions. Anyone who will profit from the institution of marriage must conduct it in the way it was instituted and arranged by God because He regulates it Himself.

DIVINE PROTOCOL FOR MARRIAGE

Marriage, by God's design, is bringing two lives together to operate and function as one.

"So, they are no longer two, but one flesh. Therefore, what God has joined together, let no one separate."

-Matthew 19:6-

There is no way two lives will become one and function as such without protocol because that will only lead to disorder and confusion. God designed marriage and the only way to make the best out of it is to follow the manufacturer's manual, which is the Bible. Anything outside this is redesigning what God has done well already and is, in a way, questioning the wisdom and correctness of God.

God, in His infinite wisdom, did not leave the running, order, and protocol of marriage in the hands of those who want to be involved; it would have been catastrophic to do so. Instead, He predetermined how things would run. He didn't leave it to run on whims or shifting feelings of those involved. In essence, choosing to go for the product (marriage) implies that you accept the order and protocols that come with it.

> It will be foolish to think that we can make the best of our matrimony if we choose to ignore the Designer's instructions.

In his book, *Divine Protocols, Principles and Protocols of God's Kingdom and Government,* Dr. Ferdinand Nweke gives an enlightening perspective on this subject. He explains:

"The divine protocols of kingdom life assign specific role and mandates - official duties - to the different members of the house. According to Webster's dictionary, a duty is "that which a person owes to another; that which a person is bound, by any natural, moral or legal obligation, to pay, do or perform... The duties of marriage are sacred, God-given and mandatory. They are not optional. They are official duties - compulsory for those who occupy the various offices in the family. In God's eyes, being a husband is not just a relationship but a sacred office, with specific duties attached to the title and office, same with being a wife. To occupy an office and then refuse

to perform the duties of the office is a deadly offence in God's sight. It then behooves prospective husbands and wives to carefully study and weigh their official duties before they enter into the office of the marital estate." – Ferdinande Nweke

ORDER OF AUTHORITY

"Now I want you to realize that the head of every man is Christ, and the head of the woman is man, and the head of Christ is God."

-1 Corinthians 11:3-

I have observed from scriptures that there is no direct punishment from God to the wife for issues between her and her husband. However, the husband does not enjoy such a luxury. The scripture prescribes consequences for a

Love isn't always "Me first"
- 1 Cor 13:5b MSG

husband not treating his wife in line with God's expectations (Malachi 2:14-15; 1 Peter 3:7). God seems to leave the husband fully in charge and responsible for his wife while He (God) is directly responsible for holding the husband accountable. The correction of the husband seems to come directly from God

THE BALANCE OF LOVE

By my understanding, the Bible teaches that the wife's submission to her husband is absolute- in all things. This biblical instruction to the wife tends to imply that God placed the wife at the mercy of the husband.

However, God, in His wisdom, put a check and balance on the husband by instructing him to love his wife. This system is God's solution to the possibility of the husband mistreating or abusing his wife. When a man loves his wife according to the prescription of Scriptures, abuse is not a possibility. This kind of love places a demand on him to live for his wife.

GOD'S STANDARD OF LOVE

When you consider the definition of love by the Bible and the standard set by Jesus' love for the Church, it is apparent that the husband has a higher responsibility. The duties of each party in a marriage relationship are clearly outlined in God's word. He has provided specific information regarding how the union should be run, so it is our responsibility to seek out and obey His word. In this way, we enjoy bliss and grace in His sight, and we live by divine protocol.

Love never gives up.
Love cares more for others than for self.
Love doesn't want what it doesn't have.
Love doesn't strut,
Doesn't have a swelled head,
Doesn't force itself on others,
Isn't always "me first,"
Doesn't fly off the handle,
Doesn't keep score of the sins of others,
Doesn't revel when others grovel,
Takes pleasure in the flowering of truth,
Puts up with anything,
Trusts God always,
Always looks for the best,
Never looks back,
But keeps going to the end,
Love never dies.
-1 Corinthians 13:4-8a, MSG-

CHAPTER FIVE

THE FUNCTIONING OF THE BODY

"From him the whole body, joined and held together by every supporting ligament, grows and builds itself up in love, as each part does its work"
Ephesians 4:16

No man naturally hates himself. A man who hates his wife hates a part of himself (Ephesians 5:29). According to Genesis Chapter two, marriage is the coming together of both the male and female personalities, which requires each of them to lose their independence to begin functioning as one body.

"...from whom the whole body, supported and held together by its ligaments and sinews, grows as God causes it to grow."

-Colossians 2:19-

THE MARRIAGE RELATIONSHIP: ANALOGY OF THE BODY

The marital relationship brings the two parties involved to become one flesh, one body. This togetherness is one of the most significant challenges in marriage: the process of the husband and wife working as one, and the how of making the two function as one entity. Let us see how this works by looking at how our body functions.

MANY PARTS FORM ONE BODY

The body is the coming together of different parts with each performing unique roles for the same goal as one. There is a mystery with the body in that it is not just physical attachments but an organic entity - a kind of connection that is beyond the obvious. The hand is not merely attached to the body; it is a part of it - functionally, emotionally, physically, spiritually, and in every sense of the word.

> In the marriage relationship, your significance lies in your role as a spouse.

As the relationship between the head and the body is not just external, so are the essential characteristics of marriage not merely superficial. It is beyond two people living together. The body does not consist of a loose attachment of members, but integral parts.

HOW THE BODY FUNCTIONS

"For just as each of us has one body with many members, and these members do not all have the same function, so in Christ we, though many, form one body, and each member belongs to all the others. We have different gifts, according to the grace given to each of us. If your gift is prophesying, then prophesy in accordance with your faith. If it is serving, then serve; if it is teaching, then teach; if it is to encourage, then give encouragement; if it is giving, then give generously; if it is to lead, do it diligently; if it is to show mercy, do it cheerfully"

-Romans 12:4-8-

EACH PART GETS ITS MEANING FROM THE BODY AS A WHOLE

I want you to think about how all this makes you more significant, not less. A body isn't just a single part blown up into something huge. It's all the different-but-similar parts arranged and functioning together.

- 1 Corinthians 12:14, MSG-

In this way, we are like the various parts of the human body. Each part gets its meaning from the body as a whole, not the other way around. A chopped-off finger, hand, or toe, no matter how strong it is, will not amount to much outside of the body. Likewise, if you are married, and you still want to live as if you are independent, a problem will arise. Why? No one part constitutes the body. In the marriage relationship, your significance lies in your role as a spouse.

A BODY FUNCTIONS BY THE WORKINGS OF MANY PARTS

"The body is a unit, though it is made up of many parts; and though all its parts are many, they form one body. So, it is with Christ."

-I Corinthians 12:12-

Even though the parts of the body are many, it is still one body. Each part performs its role, which is the reason for being a part of the body. So, the husband and wife, though different parts, are still one. And the marriage relationship only exists because of the parts, the husband and the wife. The union

The body is not just physical attachments but an organic entity – a connection that is beyond the physical.

becomes productive and meaningful only by the effective functioning of each part of the union.

THE DIFFERENT PARTS, DIFFERENT FUNCTIONS
"It's all the different-but-similar parts arranged and functioning together."

-1 Corinthians 12:14-15, MSG-

The fact that the wife and the husband are one does not mean they can do or should do the same thing or function the same way. God made them male and female, not male and male, or female and female. God designed each of them to fulfill a different role and to achieve a mutual purpose collectively. So, each person in the marriage relationship must understand his/her role in fulfilling God's purpose for the union and realize that fulfilling this unique individual role will bring about the collective well-being of the marriage.

NO PART OF THE BODY WORKS FOR ITS OWN INTEREST

This makes for harmony among the members, so that all the members care for each other.

-1 Corinthians 12:25, MSG-

In the body, the primary function of each part is to serve the others. If there is an insect in your eye, your eye can't get it out on its own. It needs the hand to deal with it. If there is a wound on the left hand, it will have to be served by the right hand. There is no selfishness in your body because every part both assists and depends on its counterparts for defense and protection.

There is no fulfillment in self-service. What makes you relevant, especially as a spouse, is what you are contributing to the whole. The reason you exist is to be a blessing. A man is sick when any part of his body is not functioning well. When you are not functioning in your role as a spouse, beware! You are opening your marriage up to infection.

THERE IS NO COMPETITION IN THE BODY

The body takes delight and derives every sense of fulfillment in the proper functioning of its members. If one part of the body is winning, the entire body is winning. Members of the body do not compete with each other. They seek to perform and fulfill their roles which, in the first place, is the essence and purpose of being part of the body.

> When you are not functioning in your role as a spouse, beware! You are opening your marriage up to infection.

Every part of your body is satisfied with what it does. Every part focuses on performing its role well. Husbands and wives are not meant to compete. Each person is unique in his or her way and does well when they are satisfied in their role and functioning effectively.

INDISPENSABILITY

No matter how small or insignificant a part looks, it remains a necessary member of the body. When something is wrong with it, it affects the entire body. The husband, as the head, is as important as the wife, the body. No matter what role a part plays, it does not nullify the importance of the other part. If you are the spouse bringing in all the money, it does not mean you are the most important spouse or that you have what it takes to do without your spouse. No one member constitutes the entire body. Whatever the role you play, you must know that it is God-ordained for the scriptures say:

"God arranged the organs in the body; each one of them, as he chose.

-1 Corinthians 12:18, RSV-

The hand did not choose to be the hand, nor did the leg decide to be the leg. It is God who arranged and decided what function each part would perform. So, whatever your role or contribution in your union, know that it is your God-arranged role.

One way to demonstrate faith in God is to accept and respond to His appointment gladly. To do otherwise is to query God's wisdom.

EACH PART IS UNIQUE

Did you know that male and female goat meat differ in taste and texture, even though they are both goats? It's true! One kind of animal is unique in taste, just because of its gender. Look at your right and left hands. They look similar, right? However, it is common knowledge that even if a person is ambidextrous, each hand functions differently. In the same vein, both the husband and the wife are of the same flesh, but they operate and present quite differently.

What makes males and females different exceeds the sex organs. Not even surgery can change who you are. Our sexuality penetrates to the deepest grains of the fabric of our personality, and the molecules of our tiniest cells.

APPOINTMENT

"But as it is, God arranged the organs in the body, each one of them, as he chose"

-1 Corinthians 12:18, RSV-

Just like none of your body parts chose which part they wanted to be in life, so it is with the husband-wife relationship. The man did not choose to be the head, nor was he consulted by the Designer before he was appointed into headship. The wife was also not made what she is by her making or because of any deficiency. There is a purpose for her creation. The Bible says,

"…God arranged the organs in the body, each one of them as he chose"

- 1 Corinthians 12:18, RSV-

"All these are inspired by one and the same Spirit, who apportions to each one individually as he wills"

-1 Corinthians 12:11, RSV-

In essence, God in His wisdom appointed the man and the woman into the role of husband and wife respectively. This role-mapping was done "as He willed" or "as He chose".

One way to demonstrate faith in God is to accept and respond to His appointment gladly. To do otherwise is to query God's wisdom. The reason we have so much confusion in the marital relationship is the lack of acceptance of God's appointed roles for us. The woman prefers something different from the one assigned by her Maker. The man wants to run away from the responsibility that comes with his position.

When you refuse to play the role of your appointment, it is not just against your spouse, but a rebellion against God who created the office, assigned the roles, and set the order. Don't struggle with your Maker. Trust Him and take your position.

NOURISH +CHERISH: WHAT A MAN DOES TO HIS BODY

For no man ever hates his own flesh, but nourishes and cherishes it, as Christ does the church.

-Ephesians 5:29, RSV-

Cherishing is an attitude, a disposition. Nourishing is an action. The word 'nourishment' means to develop, to nurture, to lift; to give someone or something what it needs to be whole. In essence, nourishment ensures that the life of a person or thing is moving in a desirable direction (as used in Ephesians 6:4). It is feeding with an all-inclusive balanced diet which will make the person grow and attain development.

> When you refuse to play the role of your appointment, it is not just against your spouse, but a rebellion against God who created the office, assigned the roles and set the order.

Just as a mother will go the extra mile to prepare a meal for her infant, adding all manner of ingredients to ensure the baby grows well, be ready to go the extra mile to ensure your spouse has what he or she needs – spirit, soul and body.

A man who hates his wife hates himself. He who loves his wife loves himself. A man who loves himself will cool his body when he is hot, warm it when he's cold, avoid pain, feed himself and attempt to satisfy his appetite. When something is wrong with any part of his body, he will attend to it and do whatever will restore it as quickly as possible. All these acts are reflective of cherishing and nurturing.

Your spouse is part of your body. Consequently, he or she must be cherished and nourished, just as you would care for yourself. When you fail to do that, you are harming your body. That is the mindset with which we can function as one body. As a husband, every morning, when I wake up, one question that should be on my mind is "How can I cherish this my body – my spouse?" The scriptures buttress this fact in the verses below:

Do not let any unwholesome talk come out of your mouths, but only what is helpful for building others up according to their needs, that it may benefit those who listen.

- Ephesians 4:29-

A married couple should focus on putting in their best to cherish each other because they are on the same team, serving the same purpose.

"The man who plants and the man who waters have one purpose, and they will each be rewarded according to their own labor. For we are fellow workers in God's service; you are God's field, God's building."

-1 Corinthians 3:8-9-

Couples who cherish each other recognize that their spouses are created in God's image, just like them, and are, therefore, of immense worth and value.

The way to take care of the body is to give it what it needs or requires, not just what is available. You must consider what is good for building up your spouse with the goal of providing nourishment.

Also, it is the responsibility of the one who is to nourish to present the nutrients in a way that will be enticing to the recipient. If a man wants people to eat beef, he must not only cook it but present it in a way that they will desire to eat it. In the same vein, it is vital to nourish your spouse in an acceptable manner – and even enticing – to him/her. It is not enough to just offer good food. A wise man will also pay attention to the manner it is served and packaged.

CHAPTER SIX

THE WIFE'S ROLE IN MARRIAGE

"For man did not come from woman, but woman from man; neither was man created for woman, but woman for man."
1 Corinthians 11:8-9

God's purpose for creating Eve was to give Adam company, a helpmeet. Eve was created to help Adam become all that God had ordained him to be. She was made for him and made to suit him. He, Adam was the reason for making Eve. His need was also the determinant of her frame. In this chapter, we examine the role of wives, God's call on the wives in a Christian marriage.

SUBMISSION

God's primary role for the wife is to help her husband, and this role can only be effectively played in the place of submission. Submission is not a popular idea, but it is not an optional one either, especially for children of God. No matter how the world feels about submission, it does not change or alter God's word and instruction as it relates to this core principle.

"Heaven and earth will pass away, but my words will never pass away"

THE PROTOCOL

-*Matthew 24:35*-

"The world and its desires pass away, but whoever does the will of God lives forever"

- *1 John 2:17*-

Wives must be especially intentional in submitting to their husbands. Much of the confusion and disaster that has characterized the marriage relationship today is traceable to man's neglect of God's instruction. This responsibility of

> God's primary role for the wife is to help her husband, and this role can only be effectively played in the place of submission.

submission is not optional, it is mandatory for everyone who has taken on the role of a wife. It doesn't mean you are inferior; it is more of an order, a divine design. We will talk later about God's will for husbands to love their wives, unconditionally just as Christ loves the Church, but wives, take heed, your submission is God's command, and it is a tool in your hand.

It is commonplace for people to believe submission equals inferiority, but it is not so. You can never be less by yielding to the God of increase and His will and purpose for your life. In fact, it takes great faith and audacity to do so. It is a privilege and an advantage to be a part of God's divine design on the earth. Pay attention to the scripture below about the place of submission in God's design of marriage and His church.

"Wives, submit yourselves unto your own husbands, as unto the Lord. For the husband is the head of the wife, even as Christ is the head of the church: and he is the savior of the body. Therefore as the church is subject unto Christ, so let the wives be to their own husbands in everything."

-Ephesians 5:22-24, KJV-

What does it mean to submit? It means to defer to another. To willingly accept or yield to another. It is subjecting everything you have to another. A wife's submission to her husband implies that she deploys everything she is and has under the leadership of her husband, just as we should when we surrender our lives to Christ.

COMPONENTS OF SUBMISSION

It is important that we talk about the components of submission. The components of submission are simple. Submission requires to elements: people or the "who" and a process- the "how".

WHO?

"Wives, submit yourselves unto your own husbands, as unto the Lord."

-Ephesians 5:22, KJV-

Wives, God is specific about whom you must submit to. You must submit to your husband, the authority in your marriage, not to every man. The marriage relationship brings in the designation of husband and wife. It is within this framework that the Bible instructs the wife to submit.

HOW?

"Wives, submit yourselves unto your own husbands, as unto the Lord."

- Ephesians 5:22, KJV-

God calls the wife to submit **as unto the Lord**. Every translation of the Holy Scripture explains this to be so. So, it is not primarily a response to your husband but first, a response to God.

"Therefore, as the Church is subject unto Christ, so let the wives be to their own husbands in everything"

Ephesians 5:24 KJV

Submission to your husband is never contingent upon his ability, character, actions, or inactions towards you. It does not matter if he deserves it or not. You are never doing him a favor when you submit to his leadership; it should be done as an act of obedience to God, who gave the instruction. It is about your reverence for God and his word.

BREADTH & SCOPE

"Therefore, as the church is subject unto Christ, so let the wives be to their own husbands in everything"

-Ephesians 5:24, KJV-

The Bible teaches that the wife should submit to her husband in all things. All things means everything, excluding nothing. This is not to demean the wife, but to ensure that there is order in the home.

CAPACITY

"For the husband is the head of the wife, even as Christ is the head of the church: and he is the savior of the body"

-Ephesians 5:23, KJV-

You are to submit to your husband in his capacity as your head. Your husband being the head means that you defer to him for direction, decision, and coordination.

"Therefore, as the church is subject unto Christ, so let the wives be to their own husbands in everything"

-Ephesians 5:24, KJV-

The 'how' of a wife's submission is fully modeled in the Christ-Church relationship. A wife is not to take clues primarily from her culture or environment but fully submit as the Church submits to Christ.

THE UNBELIEVING HUSBAND

"Wives, in the same way be submissive to your husbands so that, if any of them do not believe the word, they may be won over without words by the behavior of their wives, when they see the purity and reverence of your lives."

-1 Peter 3:1-2-

The Bible teaches that the wife should submit, even when her husband is not a believer. Note that the verse started with "…in the same way" and in other versions, "…in the same manner," and "likewise". This shows that a pattern had been established before this point. In First Peter Chapter two, the discourse is on the attitude of a believing servant towards an unbelieving master.

The example of Jesus, a righteous person suffering unjustly, was used to buttress the message to the servant (1 Peter 2:21-23). Hence, the *"in the same way" or "likewise"* in First Peter Chapter three refers to either the relationship between the godly servant and a wicked master or the pattern of the righteous Jesus suffering unjustly.

Submission to your husband is never contingent upon his ability, character, actions or inactions towards you.

These Scriptures make it apparent that the responsibility of the wife to submit does not depend on the actions of the husband.

"… Submit yourselves to your masters with all respect, not only to those who are good and considerate but also to those who are harsh."

-1 Peter 2:18-

The beauty therein is this:

"For it is commendable if a man bears up under the pain of unjust suffering because he is conscious of God … when they hurled their insults at him, he did not retaliate; when he suffered, he made no threats. Instead, he entrusted himself to him who judges justly"

-1 Peter 2:19,23-

SUBMISSION – MUTUAL OR ABSOLUTE?

Submit to one another out of reverence for Christ. Wives submit to your husbands as to the Lord. For the husband is the head of the wife as Christ is the head of the church, his body, of which he is the Savior. Now as the church submits to Christ, so also wives should submit to their husbands in everything.

-Ephesians 5:21-24-

This scripture answers the question of 'why' the wife should submit to her husband - because he is the head. And to give a proper definition to the nature and extent of the headship, the Bible provided a

Submission should be *"... in everything."*

graphic illustration of the headship of Christ over the Church, His body.

It is like saying to someone who doesn't understand the structure in the Baptist setting that the President of the Seminary is the head just as a Vice-Chancellor is the head of a university. The person will have to draw from his knowledge of the role and authority of a University Vice-Chancellor to understand the role of the Seminary President.

The scripture above also addresses the manner and extent of the submission *"... as the church submits to Christ."* So, whoever desires knowledge of this will just need to copy the submission of the Church to Christ and replicate it to her husband. To what extent should this be? Submission should be *"... in everything."* From the foregoing, the following critical points are apparent:

- The kind of submission from a wife to her husband as explained in the scripture above is absolute and will negate the principle of mutual submission mentioned in verse 21. In mutual submission, there is no order because no one is responsible; submission is left at the discretion of the parties involved.
- Nowhere else is this idea of mutual submission between the husband and wife taught in the Bible.

- In the entire Ephesians chapter 5, three relationships were addressed: Husband-Wife, Parent-children, and Master-Servant relationship. If we relate verse 21 to the husband-wife relationship, then it means it must be applied to the other two relationships discussed. However, the Bible does not suggest, in any way, that parents should submit to their own children, nor does it teach that masters should submit to their slaves.

For proper understanding, we should consider other places in the Bible where this word translated 'submit' is used.

- Jesus' submission to His parents (Luke 2:51)
- Christ being subject to God the Father. (1 Corinthians 15:28; Hebrews 12:9; James 4:7)
- Demons being subject to the apostles (Luke 10:17, 20)
- Citizens being subject to governing authorities (Romans 13:1; Titus 3:1; 1 Peter 2:13)

"And do not be drunk with wine, in which...; but be filled with the spirit, speaking to one another in psalms and hymns and spiritual songs, singing and making melody in your heart to the Lord, giving thanks always for all things to God the Father in the name of our Lord Jesus Christ, submitting to one another in the fear of God"

-Ephesians 5:19-20, NKJV-

This scripture gives several practical ways in which Christians can express being filled with the Spirit. Here, Paul brings out another - mutual submission. Submission, in the context of a Christian relationship, includes the idea of putting someone else, and their needs, above ourselves. It is apparent that Ephesians chapter 5 verse 21 addresses the relationship among believers and not that of husband and wife.

Why is God interested in this submission issue? ORDER!

Then, one might wonder, "Are husband and wife not believers? I will attempt to answer this question by way of illustration. My church service starts at 7 am. It is expected that every church member arrives at 7 am. But now the Pastor announced that henceforth, workers in the church must arrive at 6 am. There is a general rule for the 7 am but this directive will no longer guide anyone who signs up for ordination as a Church worker. Specific rules usually override general rules.

The same applies the moment a woman marries a man, takes on the role and status of a wife, the specific instruction applies. Why is God interested in this submission issue? ORDER! God wants orderliness. Order is usually not about who is right or wrong; it is about following due process.

SUBMISSION, NOT JUST ANOTHERONE OF PAUL'S TEACHINGS: NUMBERS 30

The teaching on the wife's submission is not just something Apostle Paul thought up, but a pattern we find ordained by God right from the Old Testament as seen in the book of Numbers.

"These are the regulations the Lord gave Moses concerning relationships between a man and his wife, and between a father and his young daughter still living at home"

-Numbers 30:16-

As we continue to talk about submission, wives, let's agree that submission is part of the vow you chose to make with your spouse, before God at the altar. The subject of Numbers 30 in its entirety is about a vow. The passage also illustrates a pattern: the principle of relationship and submission. I also believe that the purpose of this chapter is clarity. It is a general principle that every vow must stand and be fulfilled. A vow before God is not a small thing and as such, everyone must do everything to ensure they fulfill their vows without delay.

"When you make a vow to God, do not delay paying it; for He has no pleasure in fools. Pay what you have vowed - Better not to vow than to vow and not pay"

-Ecclesiastes 5:4-5, NKJV-

A vow is not something you can change your mind about once it is said. The clarification in Numbers 30 became necessary to give exemption to the rule which made paying of vow mandatory for certain persons who, on their own, can make a vow but because of certain limitation, in this case, a higher authority, are limited. Three categories are discussed in Numbers 30 of how binding such vows are.

A LADY UNDER THE ROOF OF HER FATHER

According to Numbers 30:3-5, a lady in her father's house is subject to her father, and as such, the father can approve or disapprove her vow. When her father disapproves, God will not hold it against her because obedience to her father takes precedence over her self-imposed religious obligation.

A WIDOW OR A DIVORCED WOMAN

"Any vow or obligation taken by a widow or divorced woman will be binding on her."

-Numbers 30:9-

The vow of a widow or a divorced woman must be fulfilled because there is no possibility of interception by anyone above her other than God because she has no male authority over her.

A WIFE

According to Numbers 30:6-8, vows of this kind falls into two categories:

- ***The vow made before marriage:*** Numbers 30:6-8 explains that if a woman made a vow before marriage, on entering into a marriage relationship, the husband has the right to review the existing vows in her life and can determine whether they stand or not.
- ***The vow made after marriage:*** Numbers 30:10-14 explains that a married woman's vow is as good as her husband will allow her to keep it.

"Her husband may confirm or nullify any vow she makes or any sworn pledge to deny herself"

-Numbers 30:13-

Where the husband exercises his authority contrary to the laid down procedure and a breach occurs, the husband is answerable for it before God. God will hold him accountable. The implication is that whether the husband goes about his disapproval rightly or wrongly, the wife is to act in line with her husband's instruction.

"He takes her guilt on himself"

-Numbers 30:15, MSG-

These vows are made to God, but He allows the husband's authority to prevail. This principle put down by God ensures order and eliminates confusion in the home. His intention is not who is right or wrong; it is about order.

BIBLICAL. NOT CULTURAL.

I have heard people say Paul's instruction to the Ephesian church was to address the cultural milieu in Ephesus that the Bible did not capture. This is far from the truth. There is no way Paul would be teaching culture to address culture. Paul, a stranger wouldn't become a teacher over the owners of the culture. Therefore, Paul's teachings were not cultural. He was simply providing a biblical,

"Like Sarah...you are her daughters if you do what is right and do not give way to fear."

1 Peter 3:6b

Christian alternative to the people. He was teaching God's perspective to the people as alternatives to what the culture of their day and place dictated.

The teaching on submission is not just in the book of Ephesians. It is taught in Colossians 3:18 where wives are instructed to be subject to their husbands. It is taught in Titus 2:4-5, 1 Timothy 2:11 and by Peter in 1 Peter 3:1-6. Peter even went further to help us see that this was not just a new teaching, but a characteristic of godly women of old. 1 Peter 3:5-6 describes perfectly the lifestyle of a wife who follows God

"For this is the way the holy women of the past who put their hope in God used to adorn themselves. They submitted themselves to their own husbands, like Sarah, who obeyed Abraham and called him her lord. You are her daughters if you do what is right and do not give way to fear."

-1 Peter 3:5-6-

JESUS: THE DEMONSTRATOR OF SUBMISSION

The headship of God is clearly demonstrated in the manner of the relationship between God and Christ. We see God use His headship, showing us a model. Christ also exemplified subjection, submitting Himself to the headship of God. The two

Jesus exemplifies the submission model.

sides of the coin- being in authority and being under authority are demonstrated in this relationship.

In Christ's headship over man, we are also left with examples and the model of what it means to be in authority. It is clear how Christ managed his authority over humanity. For example, He could have crushed the men who nailed Him to the cross. Jesus exemplifies the submission model.

"Who, being in very nature God, did not consider equality with God something to be grasped, but made himself nothing, taking the very nature of a servant, being made in human likeness. And being found in appearance as a man, he humbled himself and became obedient to death— even death on a cross!"

-Philippians 2:6-8-

"For God called you to do good, even if it means suffering, just as Christ suffered for you. He is your example, and you must follow in his steps. He never sinned, nor ever deceived anyone."

-1 Peter 2:21-22, NLT-

Jesus is God in every form (John 1:1). However, He subjected Himself to God, the Father, for the reason of order and purpose. He did not like the cross experience. It was not pleasurable to Him at all as revealed in Matthew 26:39:

"My Father, if it is possible, may this cup be taken from me. Yet not as I will, but as you will."

-Matthew 26:39b-

Even in His pain, he was committed to His Father's will. His own will was a way around the cross but in submission, he yielded to the Father's will. Submission is different from agreement. Expressing your view or reasoning things out with your husband is not necessarily a sin, as long as it is done in humility and not with contentious pride or rebellious motive. What was the result of this act of submission?

"Wherefore God also hath highly exalted him, and given him a name which is above every name: That at the name of Jesus every knee should bow, of things in heaven, and things in earth, and things under the earth; And that every tongue should confess that Jesus Christ is Lord, to the glory of God the Father"

--Philippians 2:9-11, KJV-

Jesus, by this act of submission, won God's heart and the outcome is that Jesus is now in control in a strategic way, as even God the Father now acts and responds in Jesus' name.

Fear negates God's word, and it is an indication of lack of faith

Similarly, I have seen this positive outcome of submission in marriages. Wives who have learnt the act of submission know that it is the way to take charge of their husbands. When the issue of who is in control of the home is not in contention, the husband usually leaves things to his wife.

PUT YOUR HOPE IN GOD

"… For this is the way the holy women of the past who put their hope in God used to adorn themselves. They submitted themselves to their own husbands, like Sarah, who obeyed Abraham and called him her lord. You are her daughters if you do what is right and do not give way to fear."

-1 Peter 3:5-6-

"When he was reviled, he did not revile in return; when he suffered, he did not threaten, but continued entrusting himself to him who judges justly."

-1 Peter 2:23, ESV-

"When he was insulted, he did not answer back with an insult; when he suffered, he did not threaten, but placed his hopes in God, the righteous Judge."

-1 Peter 2:23, GNT-

Believing wives are asked to emulate Sarah as a model of a godly wife. Sarah's experience with Abraham on some occasions was very unpleasant. If Sarah's name did not come up in the New Testament in this manner, many would have waved it away as an Old Testament teaching. However, Sarah is showcased in the New Testament as a model for wives to emulate. The Bible recorded at least two occasions where Sarah lied in submissiveness to Abraham: her husband putting her at risk. This experience shows that Abraham, though Father of faith, was far from being perfect; he had weaknesses. It would be wrong to insinuate that it was easy for Sarah to submit to her husband because he was such an ideal godly man.

The reason Sarah was able to submit to her husband, even at her risk, was because she put her hope in God. Both occasions when Sarah was asked to lie by her husband for his own safety put her at risk instead. However, in both instances, we saw God show up for Sarah, doing that which her husband was unable to do. Sarah's hope was not misplaced. I am not asking you to sin on behalf of your husband but to show you that a submissive wife puts her hope in God and hope in God is never misplaced.

"But the LORD sent terrible plagues upon Pharaoh and his household because of Sarai, Abram's wife."

-Genesis12:17, NLT-

"One night, however, God came to Abimelech in a dream and told him, "You are as good as dead because of the woman you have taken, for she is a married woman."... For on account of Abraham's wife Sarah, the LORD had completely closed all the wombs in Abimelech's household."

-Genesis 20:3, 18, BSB-

One of the tools the devil uses is 'fear of the unknown.' Many times, believers respond more to fear than to God. This should not be so. Fear negates God's word, and it is an indication of a lack of faith. Fear is the opposite of doing what is right. One major thing that keeps women from being submissive to their husbands is fear of the unknown, fear of the consequences of the probable bad decisions of their husbands.

It is natural to want to give in to fear but, in the Scripture above, the Bible brings in the contrast between doing what is right and giving in to fear. Being ruled by fear often leads to taking wrong decisions which are not in line with God's instructions.

FINAL WORD ON SUBMISSION

Husbands, it is the wife's responsibility to be submissive to her husband. The Bible does not teach anywhere that the husband is to force his wife to submission. It is not the husband's duty to get his wife to the place of submission. He may take this up in the place of prayer and teaching the word, but not in any physical way. It is a joyful choice the wife must make out of reverence for God.

> Being ruled by fear often leads to taking wrong decisions which are not in line with God's instructions.

Biblical submission in marriage does not mean a wife cannot express her opinion or should not have one. As a matter of fact, every husband should be glad to have a wife who helps smoothen his views with alternative opinions. Usually, having alternative views helps deepen conviction and strengthen one's view. Submission in marriage does not mean a wife should be docile, reserved, or feel inferior. A husband who does not listen to the view of his wife is missing out on one of God's greatest provisions of help for his life; "*...help comparable to him,*" as stated in Genesis 2:18. May God continue to illuminate His word for you in Jesus' name.

CHAPTER SEVEN

THE ROLE OF THE HUSBAND IN MARRIAGE

"For the husband is the head of the wife as Christ is the head of the church"
Ephesians 5:23

God has appointed every husband to two very clearly defined roles in the marriage relationship according to Ephesians 5:22-33. The two primary roles of a husband are that of a leader and that of a lover. These two roles are critical because each reflects two very important roles Jesus desires to see reflected in the Church, who has been called to lovingly and willingly submit to His authority. As we see in the scripture above, Ephesians 5:23 confirms this for us.

> Leadership is given, not for the benefit of the leader, but the benefit of the led.

THE HEAD AND LEADER

When we talk about leadership in our days, the concept of the boss-servant relationship is what tends to come to mind. However, the Bible is clear that the Kingdom brand of leadership is the model every

Christian husband should subscribe to: ...*as Christ is the head of the Church.*

The Bible gives a clear picture of how Christ leads the Church. The leadership style of Jesus is that of a servant-leader. This leadership model is practically demonstrated in His interactions with His disciples during His earthly ministry. Leadership is given, not for the benefit of the leader, but the benefit of the led. So, leadership, in Jesus' concept, is serving the led.

"For even the Son of Man did not come to be served, but to serve, and to give his life as a ransom for many"

-Mark 10:45-

"Jesus said to them, "The kings of the Gentiles lord it over them; and those who exercise authority over them call themselves, Benefactors. But you are not to be like that. Instead, the greatest among you should be like the youngest, and the one who rules like the one who serves. For who is greater, the one who is at the table or the one who serves? Is it not the one who is at the table? But I am among you as one who serves"

-Luke 22:25-27-

According to Jesus, a leader is first a servant. This is further demonstrated when Jesus washed the feet of His disciples.

"When he had finished washing their feet, he put on his clothes and returned to his place. "Do you understand what I have done for you?" he asked them. "You call me 'Teacher' and 'Lord,' and rightly so, for that is what I am. Now, that I, your Lord and Teacher, have washed your feet, you also should wash one another's feet. I have set you an example that you should do as I have done for you"

-John 13:12-15-

That powerful move is only an example of servant leadership demonstrated by our Lord and Savior. Let's look at how Jesus led as this will serve as a template for husbands:

- Teaching and instructing His disciples
- Serving His disciples
- Associating and relating with His disciples
- Delegating and giving assignments
- Being an example to His disciples

Husbands, this is the standard of leadership you must arise to take and be diligent in maintaining.

THE LOVER

"Husbands, love your wives, just as Christ loved the church and gave himself up for her"

-Ephesians 5:25-

Husbands, to love yourself is to love your wife. What does this mean? If you are a husband, your wife is a part of you. She is a member of your own body and should be treated the way you will treat other parts of your body. Treat your wife just like you would treat other parts of your body. How do you treat your legs? How do you treat your face? If you love yourself, keep that same energy of caring, strengthening, and nurturing for your wife. Ephesians 5:22-33 commands the man to love his wife in two ways:

- As himself
- As the church

"However, each one of you also must love his wife as he loves himself, and the wife must respect her husband"

-Ephesians 5:33-

As Himself

"In this same way, husbands ought to love their wives as their own bodies. He who loves his wife loves himself"

-Ephesians 5:28-

"However, each one of you also must love his wife as he loves himself"

-Ephesians 5:33-

Husbands, this truth must sink deep into your heart until it governs your actions and inactions towards your wife. On sighting Eve for the first time, Adam said:

"This is now bone of my bones and the flesh of my flesh"

-Genesis 2:23a-

This affirmation implies that the husband must relate with the wife as a part of himself. Men, once you are married, you must not ever again think of yourself in isolation since your wife is a part of you. If you do, you will be like a man who wants to access a room through the window but only considers if the right side of his body will go through and not his left side. You will end up stuck in-between and going nowhere, sir!

The husband is only a part of the union, so he must be mindful of the other part of him, his wife. When you are not considerate of your wife, you are showing hatred to yourself. When you want to enter a commercial bus, you not only think of getting a place to sit, but you also want to be sure your leg will rest well, and your head will be comfortable. No one would enter a vehicle where only a part of him will be inside and the other will drag along outside.

"After all, no one ever hated his own body, but he feeds and cares for it, just as Christ does the church"

-Ephesians 5:29-

The husband's attitude to his wife should be the same as to his body. No neglect. No abuse. When a man abuses any part of his body, all of him suffers.

AS CHRIST LOVES THE CHURCH

"Husbands, love your wives, just as Christ loved the church and gave himself up for her to make her holy, cleansing her by the washing with water through the word, and to present her to himself as a radiant church, without stain or wrinkle or any other blemish, but holy and blameless"

-Ephesians 5:25-27-

As you read here, you see that the husband is to devote himself to the purpose of his wife's wellbeing. The husband must do all to ensure that his wife lives right with God, is sanctified, and made whole. Jesus took the responsibility of making the Church what he wanted, what was acceptable to Him. The Church was far from being that which Christ wanted, but love propelled Him to do all, including sacrificing Himself, to ensure that the Church becomes that which He desires.

Love makes you take responsibility for the good of the one you love.

"Christ's love makes the church whole. His words evoke her beauty. Everything he does and says is designed to bring the best out of her,"

-Ephesians 5:27, MSG-

Husbands, you have a similar responsibility to your wife. You must labor to bring your wife to your standard under God. It is not enough to say, "My wife doesn't know how to talk," "My wife doesn't know how to cook," and so on. You must see it as your responsibility to teach and nurture her to be good. Any deficiency in your wife should be taken as an indication that you still have work to do in laboring to bring your wife to God's standard. You should take responsibility for the development of your wife's personality and character, just as Jesus sanctifies and continuously cleanses the Church.

It is also important to note that Christ does not love the Church because the Church is holy or pleasing to Him, but He labored to make her holy because He loves her. Love propels the one who loves to do all that is possible for the loved to become all that is good. The Church is not fit for Christ by nature, but Christ resolved to make her fit by grace. Love makes you take responsibility for the good of the one you love.

> The matter between you and your wife goes far beyond just the two of you.

How did Jesus achieve this? One way was through sacrifice. Love should not just be in words; it must be expressed in deeds. Sacrifice is the most significant proof of love. Christ gave Himself so that the Church can become presentable.

Another way was that He washed by the Word. Jesus cleanses His Church through the ministry of His Word (John 15:3; 17:17). The husband is to be the primary teacher of the wife. This responsibility demands that he should be ahead in knowing about God and serving Him. He should receive word from God that will bring transformation in his wife.

THE HUSBAND'S ACCOUNTABILITY TO GOD

Husbands are directly responsible and accountable to God. I consider this a fearful thing. Every husband who knows God must be concerned about this. It should make you tremble. The matter between you and your wife goes far beyond just the two of you. Being the head is not a license to be frivolous or wicked. It is a call to service with accountability. It is a trust which must not be betrayed. The authority is not your own; it is delegated.

> Being the head is not a license to be frivolous or wicked. It is a call to service with accountability. It is a trust which must not be betrayed.

Husbands, you are called to represent God in your homes. When you abuse this authority, you misrepresent the One who commissioned you. Moses missed out on God's best, all because he misrepresented God.

His action seemed simple. But as we learned, it was very significant, and it came with a grave consequence for Brother Moses:

At the desert of Zin, when Israel settled in Kadesh, there was no water and the people rebelled against Moses and Aaron. God instructed Moses to speak to the rock, but Moses instead struck the rock twice.

-Numbers 20:1-12-

As you read on later, you see God's response. He was not happy, and He did not allow Moses to step foot in the Promised Land. Did Moses have a right to be angry? Yes, the people misbehaved. They did not show faith in God. They were rebellious against God and Moses' leadership, but God did not consider that a good excuse for Moses to abuse the authority that God gave him over the people.

Men, use your God-given authority as husbands in obedience to God, not in response to the people. Learn from the error of Moses. Don't allow people to provoke you and bring you against God. God was not happy with Moses because Moses did not honor God as holy before the people. God barred Moses from the Promised Land for misrepresenting Him. Moses used His God- given authority in a manner contrary to the instructions God had given him.

Husbands who know God should be very careful how they respond to provocation from their spouses. They should be conscious of God, whom they represent, who gave them the authority over their wives and do all to act in a manner that would honor God as holy before their wives. To use your God-given authority over your wife contrary to the manner prescribed by the Giver is disrespect and dishonor to the Giver. Husbands can choose to honor or dishonor God in the exercise of their authority. You should act more in response to God than to your wife. Moses got carried away by the people's misbehavior and got into trouble with God.

CLOSED HEAVENS

"Another thing you do: You flood the Lord's altar with tears. You weep and wail because he no longer pays attention to your offerings or accepts them with pleasure from your hands.14 You ask, "Why?" It is because the Lord is the witness between you and the wife of your youth, because you have broken faith with her, though she is your partner, the wife of your marriage covenant."

- Malachi 2:13-

The consequence of unfaithfulness is enormous. It simply means the heavens are closed over such man. God no longer regards his offering, nor receives it with goodwill from his hands. Husbands, this should help you to see that it is more important to stay faithful to your wife than give offering in church. When the first one is not in place, the other is automatically affected.

So, it is better to ensure that the primary thing, being in good faith with your wife is taken care of, so that it does not make nonsense of your offerings to God - in cash and kind. No matter how big the offering is, it does not interest God. He won't accept it with pleasure except you are faithful to your wife.

It is difficult for an unfaithful husband to attract God's favor and blessing on his life. When God disregards a man's weeping and offering, it means that such a man is living under a closed heaven. The Scriptures further buttress this as it admonishes husbands to:

"…be considerate as you live with your wives and treat them with respect as the weaker partner and as heirs with you of the gracious gift of life, so that nothing will hinder your prayers."

- 1 Peter 3:7-

The weakness is of the wife, but the responsibility is on the husband. It is the wife who is weaker, but it is the husband who must show understanding and be mindful of her. It is the wife who is more fragile, but it is the husband's prayer that is at stake as a result of his handling this weakness that does not emanate from him. A wise husband will go all out to manage his wife's weakness in such a way that it does not constitute hindrances between him and God. Verse 16 of Malachi chapter 2 brings another dimension to this concept:

"The man who hates and divorces his wife," says the Lord, the God of Israel, "does violence to the one he should protect," says the Lord Almighty. So be on your guard, and do not be unfaithful."

-Malachi 2:16-

Your wife is yours to protect. It is your responsibility to ensure she lives fine. It amounts to an act of irresponsibility to put aside the one whom you are meant to protect. It is a dereliction of duty. A man who hates and divorces his wife does violence to the very one he should protect. To protect means to keep safe from harm or injury. So, nurture, protect and care for your wife. It is your duty.

GOD AS A WITNESS

"You ask, "Why?" It is because the LORD is the witness between you and the wife of your youth. You have been unfaithful to her, though she is your partner, the wife of your marriage covenant."

-Malachi 2:14-

"Yet you say, "For what reason? "Because the LORD has been a witness between you and the wife of your youth, with whom you have dealt treacherously; Yet she is your companion and your wife by covenant"

-Malachi 2:14, NKJV-

Another fearful thing about the role of the husband is the fact that God Himself is the witness; He is the Referee and there is no hiding place. Can you imagine what it is for the All-knowing God, Omniscient, to act as a witness against one? He knows your motives and secrets, sees into your heart and intentions, and can never be fooled. Your Pastor may be deceived by your words, pretentious acts, and cover-up deeds, but the One who is a Witness in this matter cannot. This is the nature of the role that God has placed on the husband, and it demands seriousness and responsibility.

You should act more
in response to God
than to your wife.

CHAPTER EIGHT

THE CHRISTIAN MARRIAGE: THE WAY OF THE CROSS

"Wives, submit yourselves to your own husbands as you do to the Lord. For the husband is the head of the wife as Christ is the head of the church, his body, of which he is the Savior."
Ephesians 5:22-23

We must understand marriage as a divine institution and as such, we can only enter to live it, not to reconstruct it. The design, terms, and structure are given by the One (God) who instituted it. So, to get married is to enter an institution that is already established, with a clearly defined structure.

Ephesians 5:22-33 contains clear instructions for the relationship between husbands and wives. The following insights are essential for our application of these instructions.

INSIGHTS FROM EPHESIANS 5

These instructions are God's word to you, your spouse is only a recipient, a person on whom you apply the instructions. It is a matter primarily between you and God, the Giver of the instruction.

Your spouse is not the one you are obeying or disobeying. When you focus too much on your spouse and not the Giver of the instruction, you may end up finding yourself opposed to God.

These instructions to husbands and wives are mutually exclusive. One does not depend on the other. The directive to the husband is not dependent on the one to the wife, nor is the one to the wife dependent on specific actions from the husband. God's word to

> When you focus too much on your spouse and not the Giver of the instruction, you may end up finding yourself opposed to God.

you is not dependent on your spouse. Loving your wife is not subject to her being submissive to you. Your submission as a wife is not dependent on your husband showing you love. You are responsible and accountable for your part of the instructions.

Please understand that these God-given instructions are definite. They are not left at your discretion. You are not to take the definition of love from your culture. The parameters are clearly stated, "… as Christ loved the Church" (Ephesians 5:25). This means to the same degree, amount, or extent to which Christ loves the Church. Essentially, Christ is the standard. He is the model. The scope of your submission as a wife is not to be taken from the world system. It is *"… as the church submits to Christ"* (Ephesians 5:24). The picture painted in the relationship between Christ and the Church should be correctly understood and followed.

The issue of marriage is a mystery (Ephesians 5:32). You need to seek to live it more than you seek to understand it. The more you live it, the better you understand it, and the more you see it expressed in you. The fullness of marriage is made manifest in your togetherness. The potentials and the blessings are great, but they are only expressed and manifested in your coming together.

CHRISTIAN MARRIAGE: THE WAY OF THE CROSS

There is a tendency to think that God is partial, that His demands and responsibility allocation are one-sided or that one person is more favored than the other in the marriage relationship. My first response to that thinking pattern would be:

"Does the clay say to him who fashions it, 'What are you making?' or 'Your work has no handles'?"

-Isaiah 45:9b, RSV-

For both husband and wife, the example is Christ, and the pattern is the cross; and that is what God has called Christian marriages to emulate.

Thinking that God favors one over the other in the context of marriage will amount to questioning God's wisdom. It will be a vote of 'No Confidence' in God's faithfulness and wisdom. However, an in-depth look at the scriptures shows that God's demand on both husband and wife is not short of the way of the cross. Christian marriage is the way of the cross. Some women view submission as demeaning. Women may feel jealous of men and wonder why the Bible would ask them to be submissive to men. But this situation is just like wondering why the name of Jesus is everywhere; the Bible says that Jesus learned obedience through the things He suffered. Christ is the model for the husband and the wife; His pattern to be followed is the way of the cross.

> Love can never truly exist without giving. Love gives, gives and gives.

For both husband and wife, it is apparent that the example is Christ, and the pattern is the cross; and that is what God has called Christian marriages to emulate. To the husbands, the Bible says, "… *love your wives, just as Christ loved the church*" (Ephesians 5:25). This model is the standard for husbands—to love as Christ loves the Church. The how of submission and love set out in the Bible are nothing short of the way of the cross. The husband is to love like Christ loved the Church and gave Himself up to die on the cross in place of the Church. The wife is to submit in "like manner" that Christ submitted unto death even while he was not guilty (1 Peter 3:1).

The Bible says that husbands should love their wives as Christ loves the Church. How does Christ love the Church? If, as a husband, you want to meet God's standard and fulfill God's demand over your life, all you need do is look at how Christ loves the Church and emulate it. Consider what Christ has done for the Church and replicate it with your wife.

CHRIST'S STANDARD OF LOVE FOR HUSBANDS

According to Ephesians 5:25-30, there are three evident characteristics of Christ's standard of love.

THE LOVE OF CHRIST IS SACRIFICIAL

According to Ephesians 5:25b, sacrifice means giving up something valuable with the possibility of gaining something else of value or avoid an even more significant loss. Succinctly, it is giving up oneself for another. In practical terms, sacrifice means that if someone wants to take the wife for an offense she has committed, the husband should be willing to offer himself in place of the wife. It implies that if there is danger, and such a threat must take one person, the husband is to face such a risk while the wife is secured.

Sacrifice is giving up your rights for your wife to enjoy. The love of Christ for the Church is sacrificial; He gave. Love can never truly exist without giving. Love gives, gives, and gives.

The kind of love which the husband is called to give is sacrificial, at his expense. The sacrifice being referred to can cost the life of a man, and so loving your wife as Christ loves the Church implies that you value her life even more than yours just as Christ gave up Himself and gave up His rights.

When the Church needed the blood of Christ to be all that it should be, Jesus gave the blood. Hence, for a husband, the call to love is to walk in the path of the cross because it makes your wife's life more valuable to you than yours.

THE CHRIST KIND OF LOVE IS SANCTIFYING

Read Ephesians 5:26-28 as it covers the significance of sanctification. The word "sanctify" means to set apart and the following are the implications as it relates to the husband-wife relationship:

- Husbands have to set themselves apart wholly and only for their wives. Anything contrary to that is a sin. Set apart the totality of yourself for your wife.
- The husband is called to make his wife clean, perfect, and acceptable. This call requires investment. Ephesians 5:26b says, "*...by the washing with water through the word"* and this means that if she is dirty, you take up the responsibility to clean her up.

Sanctifying means cleansing or bringing to a level of perfection, and the responsibility is on the one sanctifying to bring up unto an acceptable level of perfection. What does this imply? If your wife doesn't know how to read, but you can read, sanctification demands that you teach her and labor to bring her to that level. Hence, the kind of love that Christ has for the Church demands that you do everything to bring up your wife from the level she is to where she is meant to be. If your wife does not know how to cook or speak properly, sanctify her by teaching and helping her.

The example of Jesus illustrates that the way to sanctify is by the word. Husbands must teach their wives and feed them with the word of God because it is critical and essential; this is the only way to build up your wife and help her grow - the word of God.

89

THE CHRIST KIND OF LOVE IS SATISFYING

Take your time to read Ephesians 5:28-30. Husbands are instructed to love their wives in such a way that brings satisfaction. How should a man love his wife? He should love his wife as he loves himself. Everyone wants satisfaction

> Husbands have to set themselves apart wholly and only for their wives. Anything that is contrary to that is a sin.

and because it is your body, you want to give yourself what you want. It is not just to love for the sake of loving; it is not just to 'fulfill righteousness'. When a man is not satisfied, he keeps doing and giving more.

This kind of love must be given in a way that is satisfying and fulfilling. It can be achieved with a mindset of nourishing and cherishing your spouse. As explained in earlier chapters, nourishing gives satisfaction.

"LIKEWISE" FOR WIVES

"Wives, likewise, be submissive to your own husbands"

-1 Peter 3:1a, NKJV-

The responsibility God places on the wife is a call to submission. How should the wife submit? "… likewise, in the same manner…"

Slaves, submit yourselves to your masters with all respect, not only to those who are good and considerate, but also to those who are harsh. For it is commendable if a man bears up under the pain of unjust suffering because he is conscious of God. But how is it to your credit if you receive a beating for doing wrong and endure it? But if you suffer for doing good and you endure it, this is commendable before God. To this you were called, because Christ suffered for you, leaving you an example, that you should follow in his steps. He committed no sin, and no deceit was found in his mouth. When they hurled their insults at him, he did not retaliate; when he suffered, he made no threats. Instead, he entrusted himself to him who judges justly.

-1 Peter 2:18-24-

The preceding verses to 1 Peter chapter three verse one discuss the issue of submission. Slaves were instructed regarding their relationships with their masters. They were admonished to follow the example of Christ.

"...likewise, be submissive to your own husbands."

-1 Peter 3:1a, NKJV-

The word "likewise" as used here and in relation to the preceding scriptures can only mean one of two things: wives are expected to submit as slaves submit to their masters, or "as Christ submitted".

A godly wife does not retaliate. A loving and Christ-like husband does not insult or maltreat his wife.

A careful study of the focal scripture shows that the two statements mean the same thing. Slaves are instructed to adopt the pattern set by Jesus in their relationship with their masters, even in the face of persecution. This statement implies that Jesus Christ is the ultimate example to follow.

Hence, whether wives choose to follow the instruction given to slaves or Christ's example, the bottom line is that they follow Christ's model of submission which does not depend on the attitude or personality of their husbands.

A wife's submission to her husband is not dependent on his being perfect or considerate. Even if the husband is harsh, the wife is expected to submit according to 1 Peter 2:18. Whether the man is kind or inconsiderate; the wife submits by following Christ's example, not because of her husband's kindness.

NO RETALIATION

"When they hurled their insults at him, he did not retaliate; when he suffered, he made no threats. Instead, he entrusted himself to him who judges justly."

-1 Peter 2:23-

A godly wife does not retaliate. A loving and Christ-like husband does not insult or maltreat his wife because that is not the way of Christ. However, if a woman is married to a husband who is insulting or harsh, according to Christ's model of submission, she should not retaliate by being insulting in return.

"...never answered back when insulted; when he suffered, he did not threaten to get even; he left his case in the hands of God who always judges fairly."

-1 Peter 2:23, TLB-

A godly wife does not threaten to get even but entrusts herself to Him who judges justly. Her case is not in her mouth; she places her case before God, the Just Judge, who can fight her cause beyond human efforts. A wise wife leaves her matter in the hand of God who knows and can do all things. Wives must learn how to reach their husbands through God because He owns every heart.

Nobody can guide or change the heart of your husband as God can. A wise woman entrusts her case to God. There is no need to argue or fight- just go on your knees and ask God to take charge. I believe so much in the efficacy of prayer. A lot of things can be achieved without sweat in the place of prayer.

No Rights

He personally carried the load of our sins in his own body when he died on the cross so that we can be finished with sin and live a good life from now on. For his wounds have healed ours!

-1 Peter 2:24, TLB-

Christian marriage, the way of the cross is not a place of rights. A Christian who wants to claim his/her rights should not bother about marriage because when you get married, it can be likened to crucifying yourself. You can no longer insist on your line of thought or your way of doing things. And you must be open-minded to understand that when you agree to follow your spouse's idea or opinion, sometimes, things will not turn out as expected. When things happen this way, a godly woman does not take a stand of, "But I told you so" or "We should have done it my way."

Wives, fit in with your husbands' plans; for then if they refuse to listen when you talk to them about the Lord, they will be won by your respectful, pure behavior. Your godly lives will speak to them better than any words.

-1 Peter 3:1, TLB-

Marriage the way of the cross causes one to suffer for the foolishness of the other. When a wife advises her husband against an action and the husband stubbornly carries it out, if it backfires, the wife should not feel justified to ridicule her husband. She bears the sins of her husband with him without an attitude of self-righteousness. He will see his errors and see things more clearly by her respectful, pure behavior.

If you want to hold on to your rights, marriage is not a place to consider. Following the way of the cross in Christian marriage is a place of giving up one's rights and living for another. However, it is a win-win situation because that is the only way you can experience true fulfillment in marriage. Submission is not slavery and should never be considered as such because that is the example set for us by Christ. Doing it joyfully brings joy, peace, and fulfillment.

> A lot of things can be achieved without sweat in the place of prayer.

For one is regarded favorably (is approved, acceptable, and thankworthy) if, as in the sight of God, he endures the pain of unjust suffering. [After all] what kind of glory [is there in it] if, when you do wrong and are punished for it, you take it patiently? But if you bear patiently with suffering [which results] when you do right and that is undeserved, it is acceptable and pleasing to God.

-1 Peter 2:19-20, AMP-

According to this scripture, it is commendable if a person bears up under the pain of unjust suffering. Unjust suffering means that you are suffering but enduring it patiently, not because it is deserved, but because you want to obey God. If you suffer from following God, it is commendable, meaning it has God's approval. By inference, not patiently enduring when one suffers unjustly for obeying God can bring God's displeasure. Man's displeasure is challenging enough. Experiencing God's disapproval is only best imagined.

It is commendable that you suffer for desiring to follow God's standards, not for lack of alternatives, but seeing options and still choosing to stick with God. It gives God pleasure and when God is pleased, you reap the benefits thereof. Submit to your husband, take charge in the place of prayers and endure patiently, as you see the answers to your prayers unfold in God's way and at His time. The only way to truly live and gain true marital fulfillment as a Christian husband or wife is to follow the way of the cross.

ABOUT THE AUTHOR

I want to be free from every entanglement of sin and all that hinders me from being the best for Jesus. So intimate in my relationship with God that HE can make the most of me, I want to be completely abandoned for HIM showing forth His glory and maintaining an ever-increasing fellowship with HIM"

— Ayo Olaleye

Ayo Olaleye is a privileged beneficiary of God's grace in every area of his life. He and his wife, Titi, have been building a loving and growing marriage since 2006. They are committed to ministering to marriages and families and have devoted their time and resources to it. Together, they founded and coordinate Family Resource Ministry.

Ayo, a Chartered Estate Surveyor and Valuer, holds a Master of Divinity from The Nigerian Baptist Theological Seminary, Oyo State, Nigeria, a Master of Business Administration from Nasarawa State University, Nasarawa State, Nigeria, and a Master of Art in Organizational Leadership from Development Associates International. He is a fellow of the Stephen Olford Institute of Biblical Preaching, USA. Ayo, with his wife, and their children reside in Abuja, Nigeria.

www.ingramcontent.com/pod-product-compliance
Lightning Source LLC
LaVergne TN
LVHW041202080426
835511LV00006B/705